4/24

The ALEXANDER HAMILTON
You Never Knew

BY JAMES LINCOLN COLLIER

Children's Press®
A Division of Scholastic Inc.
New York Toronto London Auckland Sydney
Mexico City New Delhi H
Danbury, Connecticut

Library of Congress Cataloging-in-Publication Data

Collier, James Lincoln, 1928-
   The Alexander Hamilton you never knew / James Lincoln Collier;
illustrations by Greg Copeland.—1st American ed.
      p. cm.
Summary: Explores the childhood, character, and influential events that
shaped the life of Alexander Hamilton, one of America's founding fathers.
Includes bibliographical references and index.
   ISBN 0-516-24345-4 (lib. bdg.)   0-516-25834-6 (pbk.)
   1. Hamilton, Alexander, 1757-1804—Juvenile literature. 2. Statesmen—
United States—Biography—Juvenile literature. 3. United States—
History—Revolution, 1775-1783—Juvenile literature. 4. United States—
Politics and government—1783-1809—Juvenile literature. [1. Hamilton,
Alexander,
1757-1804. 2. Statesmen.] I. Copeland, Greg, ill.
II. Title.
   E302.6.H2C64 2003
   973.4'092—dc21

                            2003005249

Illustrations by Greg Copeland
Book design by A. Natacha Pimentel C.

Photographs © 2003: Art Resource, NY: 7 (Giraudon), 30 (Museum of the
City of New York, New York, NY, USA/Scala), cover, 4, 65 (National Portrait
Gallery, Smithsonian Institution), 46 (Réunion des Musées Nationaux), 62
(Snark); Bridgeman Art Library International Ltd., London/New York: 9, 10
(British Library, London, UK), 11 (Christie's Images, London, UK), 1, 34, 50
(Museum of the City of New York, USA), 13 (Yale Center for British Art,
Paul Mellon Collection, USA); Library of Congress: 57; National Gallery of
Art, Washington, DC: 48 (photo by Richard Carafelli); North Wind Picture
Archives: 28, 38, 39, 40, 43, 51, 55, 58, 59, 61, 66, 68; The Art
Archive/Picture Desk: 20, 33, 54, 69 (Chateau de Blerancourt/Dagli Orti), 23
(Maritime Museum Kronborg Castle Denmark/Dagli Orti).

CONTENTS

Chapter 1

BORN POOR

ALEXANDER HAMILTON WAS ONE OF the great men of American history. There is a college named for him. There is a statue of him in the heart of America's financial district in New York City. His face is on our ten-dollar bills. Some forty cities, towns, and counties in the United States are named Hamilton. Most Americans know that Alexander Hamilton is one of our most important men. But hardly anyone knows why.

This famous portrait of Alexander Hamilton shows a very determined look, which suggests his drive to climb up from the bottom.

We should, for Hamilton, possibly more than anyone except George Washington, worked out some of the most important principles in the American system. Without Hamilton's work the United States might be a quite different place to live today.

Hamilton's story is well worth telling for its own sake. It is the story of an orphan who grew up with nothing but a few worn pieces of clothing. Through brains and determination he became one of the most important men of his time.

We do now know nearly as much about Hamilton's youth as we would like to. He died fairly young, and did not live long enough to write his own story, as many elder statesmen do. We are not sure exactly where he was born, or even when. He was certainly born on one of the islands known as the Lesser Antilles, which form a kind of fence dividing the Caribbean Sea from the Atlantic Ocean.

The Lesser Antilles had been discovered by Christopher Columbus and other early European explorers at the end of the 1400s and the beginning of the 1500s. The Europeans had quickly taken them over from the Indians who lived there. Their conquest was made easier by the European diseases they brought with them, which the Indians were not used to. Many died from illnesses like smallpox and measles. The Europeans killed or enslaved most of the rest. Soon they controlled the Lesser Antilles and other Caribbean islands. These islands were claimed by various European powers, especially the English, French, Dutch, and Danish.

This sixteenth-century map of the Caribbean and portions of North America was made at a time when the New World was still largely unexplored by Europeans, although of course well known to the Indians who lived there. The islands shown here were already becoming important sources of wealth for Europeans.

The Europeans had come looking for gold, silver, and precious stones. They did not find much of these in the West Indies, as the Caribbean Islands were known. However, they soon learned that certain valuable crops grew very well in the moist tropical climate of the islands. One such crop was tobacco. The Indians had been pipe smokers for ages. The Europeans picked up the habit from them, and soon smoking was very popular in Europe. Very quickly planters in the West Indies began to make fortunes by growing tobacco for shipment to Europe.

Even more profitable was sugar. Sugarcane would not grow in Europe because the climate was too cold. Before the 1500s Europeans mainly used honey as a sweetener for food. When they learned about sugar from the Tropics they seized upon it. Particularly in the 1700s, Europeans were discovering coffee, tea, and chocolate, which also could only be grown in warm, moist climates. These drinks needed sugar. By Alexander Hamilton's birth, the West Indies were blanketed in sugarcane plantations.

These plantations were worked mainly by black slaves brought from Africa. Some of these slaves were captured by European slavers, but in most cases they were sold to the Europeans by various African chiefs in exchange for guns, rum, and other manufactured goods the Africans prized. On many Caribbean islands the black slaves outnumbered their white masters by ten or twenty to one, and had to be kept in line by harsh treatment.

Slaves cut sugarcane on the island of Antigua. This painting was made several decades after Hamilton's youth in the Caribbean, but sugar-making methods had changed little.

It was possible for a tough, aggressive man with little except brains, hard work, and luck to make a fortune in the islands. The fastest way to wealth was by growing sugar, but it was a very risky business. Drought and hurricanes often destroyed the crops. Tropical illnesses, like yellow fever, which we no longer fear, killed rich and poor alike.

But there were other ways to make a lot of money. For one thing, sugarcane was so profitable that no land was spared for growing food or pasturing cattle and hogs. It made more financial sense to use your land for sugarcane and import your food from elsewhere. In fact, a lot of food brought into the West Indies came from what would be the United States, so that American farmers, merchants, and shippers earned good money at second hand from the sugar trade.

A city or town port would have wharves to which sailing ships could tie up. In small settlements such as this one, barrels of sugar and rum had to be rolled into a small boat, which was then rowed out to the waiting ships.

Thus, many men came to the islands not to grow sugar, but to be merchants. They built shops, stores, and warehouses to sell everything that anyone on the island needed, from nails to nightgowns, beer to beef.

Although towns like Christiansted on St. Croix, where Hamilton worked as a clerk, had indoor stores, in many places outdoor markets were common. Here, wealthy ladies shop for linen, widely used for clothing and other purposes in hot climates.

Throughout the Caribbean there was a get-rich-quick atmosphere. In the towns, sugar millionaires swaggered through the streets in fine clothing along with black slaves, gamblers, smugglers, and sailors on leave spending their pay. People broken in health or fortune wheedled pennies from passersby. Everything was a gamble: you might be riding in a fine carriage one day, begging in the streets the next.

This was the world into which Alexander Hamilton was born. It was not a safe, secure world, but a rough place filled with cruel and greedy men, disease, and a sometimes violent climate. One of the lessons this world taught Alexander Hamilton was that even the lowest of the low could rise into fame and fortune quickly and spectacularly. It was a world calling for daring and ambition.

Hamilton may have been born on the tiny island of Nevis. His mother was named Rachel. She was of French descent. She grew up poor, drifting with her own mother from one little island to the next, looking for ways to make their living. When she was quite young Rachel was married and soon divorced. According to the law of that time and place, she could not remarry. However, she began living as husband and wife, without actually getting married, to a Scotsman named James Hamilton.

It is critical to this story that James Hamilton had fallen low. He had come from a quite wealthy and aristocratic Scottish family. He had grown up in a castle surrounded by gardens, lawns, and parks. Servants made his bed for him as a boy and served him his meals. People in the nearby town bowed to his father and called him sir. James Hamilton grew up believing that he was above most other people.

Unfortunately for him, he was the fourth of four sons. At that time the rule in the British Isles was that the first son inherited the land, the house, and most of the money. That may seem unfair, but it meant that the fortunes of wealthy people stayed intact and created a strong ruling class. Usually careers were arranged for younger sons as officers in the military, in politics, in law, or as church officials.

Many of the adventurers to the Caribbean remained poor, but some made great fortunes. They built grand houses, owned fine horses, and kept many servants. Here, a wealthy planter and his wife walk around their estate while a servant follows to wait on them if necessary.

So, James Hamilton should have had a good career, perhaps as a colonel in the army or an important government official. We do not know what went wrong. Possibly he disgraced himself in some manner. Perhaps he failed at several jobs and the family gave up on him. Whatever happened, he ended up in the West Indies like so many other desperate men, looking for a way to make a fortune. He did not find it. Instead, he managed to make a poor living clerking in the stores of various merchants.

He and Rachel had two children, James and Alexander, who was probably born in 1757, although some historians believe he was born two years earlier. For several years the little family drifted through the islands as the father went from job to job, always hoping to improve himself and never succeeding. The young boys, James and Alexander, dressed in shabby clothes, lived in small houses with little furniture, at times making their beds on the floor. Around them they could see people of great wealth, whose children had fine clothing, their own ponies, even their own servants.

Alexander Hamilton grew up with a sense that he had been thrown down from his rightful place. He was the grandson of a rich man who owned a castle. In Alexander's opinion, he was by rights an aristocrat. Why should he have to wear shabby clothes and sleep on floors? This sense that he was high born would haunt Alexander Hamilton throughout his life. He was very particular that people should treat him with respect and dignity. His pride was easily injured, and he was always seeing insults when no insult was intended.

Once, later on, when Hamilton was an assistant to George Washington during the American Revolution, he happened to keep Washington waiting for a few minutes. Washington sometimes had an explosive temper, and he blew up at Hamilton. "Colonel Hamilton," he roared, "You have kept me waiting at the head of the stairs these ten minutes. I must tell you, Sir, you treat me with disrespect."

Hamilton was startled, as he felt he had done nothing wrong. But his pride was badly injured. He replied, "I am not conscious of it, Sir, but, since you have thought it necessary to tell me so, we must part." Consider: Hamilton was a relatively unimportant young man, Washington was the commander of the revolutionary army and one of his nation's greatest men. Most people in Hamilton's place would have accepted Washington's criticism and let the whole thing go. Hamilton could not. Washington tried to smooth the argument over, but the proud Hamilton would not bend, and for a time relations between the two were strained. This stubborn pride, which would last Hamilton's life, grew up in the poor boy in shabby clothes who felt he ought to have been an aristocrat.

In 1765 the wandering little family landed on the island of St. Croix, today part of the American Virgin Islands and popular with vacationing Americans. Not long afterward Alexander's parents separated. We are not sure why. It may have been that Rachel was tired of the fact that James Hamilton was not able to make a decent living for her and the children. We do not know. But James gradually drifted away, and soon Alex saw his father for the last time.

We might think that Alex would be angry with his father for his failures, and then for leaving. That is not the case. All his life Alex felt sorry for his father, and sometimes wrote to him. He appeared to believe that James's misfortunes were due to bad luck rather than his own weaknesses. His father was, after all, Alex's link to the upper class, and he wanted to think well of him.

Alex's mother, Rachel, did what many people in the islands were always doing: she opened a small store. This was reasonably easy to do: you bought some goods—cloth, thread, glassware, buttons, anything else—on credit. If you could sell your goods at a profit you could gradually build up your trade. Alex, now ten, worked in the store, waiting on customers, going on errands, making deliveries.

In those days there were no free public schools. Parents had to pay for their children to go to private schools, and only the wealthy could afford to do so. But Alexander Hamilton believed he was by rights a member of the upper class, an aristocrat. Boys from such families were educated so they could have careers in business, law, the military. Alex was determined to be one of them. He would educate himself if necessary.

His mother apparently spoke French, and Alex learned the language as a child. This proved to be a great advantage later on, when the French were helping the Americans in the Revolution, for Hamilton could negotiate with the French for Washington.

Alex had been taught to read, probably by his mother, at an early age. He began reading as much as he could in his spare time. By age ten there were thirty-four books in the house, quite a large number for a poor family of the time. He worked hard at learning mathematics, read a lot of poetry, studied some chemistry and undoubtedly much history.

Most critically, he learned good handwriting. In a day before typewriters, much less computers, everything had to be written out by hand—letters, accounts, bills, even whole books. People's handwriting had to be clear and understandable. A gentleman or lady was expected to have elegant, beautiful handwriting—one to be used in business, one for personal letters, one for official papers, and such. Alex worked hard at his handwriting and became good at it.

Of all of his studies, however, what interested young Alexander Hamilton most was military history. He loved reading about great battles and their heroes, like the famous Roman general Julius Caesar, William the Conqueror of England, and no doubt Alexander the Great. As we shall see, he wanted, more than anything else, to be a military hero.

So, gradually Alex began turning himself into the gentleman he felt he ought to be. Then, in 1768, when he was about eleven, his mother caught one of the tropical fevers that abounded in the islands. Soon Alex was sick, too. A doctor was called in, but in those days nobody really understood what caused these infectious diseases, much less how to cure them. Alex recovered, but his mother died. Somebody lent Alex and his brother enough money so that they would have decent shoes for their mother's funeral. Although still a boy, Alex would now have to become a grown-up.

Chapter 2
SOME HELPFUL SPONSORS

THE LIST OF RACHEL'S POSSESSIONS that was made after she died gives some idea of how poor Alex Hamilton was. She owned some slaves, which she had been renting out to wealthier people, but slaves were plentiful in the islands and cheap; renting them did not bring much money. She also owned fourteen plates, eleven cups and saucers, four dresses, one hat, some spoons, and one bed. One bed: the boys slept on the floor.

European demand for sugar was huge. Any amount produced could be sold for a good price. As a consequence, ships like these were constantly moving around the Caribbean, bringing in manufactured goods like furniture and tools, and taking away sugar.

The boys were entrusted by the courts to a distant relative who had money. After a little more than a year he committed suicide over private problems. Under the laws of the time, the government could claim the wealth of a suicide. The boys were now on their own. Alex was probably twelve, thrown out into what he later described as "this selfish and rapacious world."

But if he owned nothing but his few clothes, he had other things of great value: high intelligence, a willingness to work hard, a determination to rise, and charm. People took to Alex—or "Ham," as they were now beginning to call him.

We must understand that in those days young men rose through what was called *preferment*. (Women were then rarely allowed into professions and other responsible jobs.) Preferment was the system by which older men in positions of some authority looked around for beginners whom they might help out. In this way they would over time place people who owed them favors in business, government, the professions. Today this would seem like favoritism and would be frowned upon, but in Hamilton's time it was the accepted way for a young man to rise. A youth like Hamilton—really still a boy—needed to attach himself to men who could help him. This Hamilton set about doing; and because he was intelligent, ambitious, and a hard worker, men came to his support.

But there was another side to it, as we have seen in the case of George Washington: Hamilton's pride, which made him fear a "personal dependence" on anyone. Perhaps the way his father had let him down so often made him afraid to trust others for help. However it happened, Hamilton did not like the idea of being beholden to anyone.

Nonetheless, without the help of an older man he would go nowhere. It was not long before he found one. His mother had bought a lot of the goods she had sold in her store from a new export-import firm, run by a family named Cruger. The Cruger firm was no small-time operation, but was headquartered in New York and had branches in London and the Caribbean islands of Jamaica, Curaçao, and St. Croix. Various Cruger brothers ran the operations in the different cities. The man in charge in Christiansted, the chief city of St. Croix, was twenty-five-year-old Nicholas Cruger.

Christiansted, where Hamilton learned the business, in 1837. Although the town has grown up a good deal since Hamilton's day, buildings like the one at left can still be found there. The harbor remains busy, but with tourist ships rather than sugar vessels.

At the time, of course, both travel and communication were slow. Letters, bills, price lists, and orders might take weeks to come by sailing ship from Europe to St. Croix, and a week or two from the firm's New York headquarters. As a result, young Cruger could not always consult with headquarters, but had to make decisions on his own about what to buy, what prices to charge, and other matters. He was buying and selling anything he could make a profit on—rice, tobacco, cloth, horses, mules, and, regrettably, slaves. He thus often had to make decisions involving large amounts of money. The risks were plentiful. You had to worry if the ship you were using would sink in a storm, be attacked by pirates, be held up by bad weather so that perishable goods were spoiled.

Nicholas Cruger knew Alex and recognized his worth. He brought him into the firm. Very quickly Alex turned himself into Cruger's right-hand man. Cruger began to place astonishing trust in his young assistant. Soon Hamilton was writing to a friend, "I contemn the groveling condition of a clerk . . . to which my fortune, etc. condemns me, and would willingly risk my life, though not my [reputation], to exalt my station . . . I'm confident, Ned, that my youth excludes me from any hopes of [rising immediately], but I mean to prepare . . . for futurity." This was a twelve-year-old boy writing.

A year after Alex joined the firm, Cruger got sick and went to New York for treatment, where he could get better doctors than he could find in the islands. He left Alex in charge.

That November there arrived in Christiansted a new sloop, which the Cruger firm had invested in. The sloop was loaded with merchandise. Hamilton went on board, looked at the cargo, and decided which of it to have unloaded for sale in St. Croix—cornmeal, lumber, barrels of apples, strings of onions, and more. He then ordered the sloop's captain to proceed to the firm's office in Curaçao with the rest of the cargo. He told the captain, "Remember, you are to make three trips this season and unless you are very diligent, you will be too

late, as our crops will be early in." And he gave the captain a letter for the head of the office in Curaçao that said, "Give me leave to hint . . . that you cannot be too particular in your instructions to [the captain]. I think he seems rather to want experience in such voyages." Then, while Cruger was still away, Hamilton decided that the firm's lawyer was not good enough. He fired him and hired another lawyer. Hamilton was fourteen years old.

People around St. Croix were beginning to notice Alex. Then, in 1772, when Alex was fifteen, a hurricane struck St. Croix. The winds howled, lightning flashed, rain drove horizontally into people's faces like pebbles. Houses were swept into rubble, burying families inside under masses of broken boards and furniture. The screams of the wounded and dying were blown away in the roaring winds.

Alex had always liked to write, and he had already composed a few light poems. Now he wrote a description of the hurricane filled with the high-flown phrases that were popular at the time. The dead had been "snatched into eternity unexpecting," brought low by "fiery meteors flying about in the air." The article was published in a local newspaper and attracted a lot of attention, especially as the writer was still a teenager.

By now it was occurring to Nicholas Cruger and a few other businessmen around St. Croix that something ought to be done for this brilliant youth. The article on the hurricane was convincing evidence that Alex was more talented than most boys of his age. Cruger and the others decided to send him to North America to get an education. They put together some money and arranged for one of Cruger's business associates in New York City to look after Alex. In June 1773, Alexander Hamilton arrived in New York to start the adventure that would be his new life.

It was an extraordinary time to be New York, for a drama was about to be played out in North America that would change the history of the world. At the time, as students of history know, the United States did not exist. There were instead thirteen individual colonies running from Georgia to what is now Maine along the Atlantic seaboard, all belonging to England. The colonies elected their own legislatures, but their governors were usually Englishmen appointed by the English government. In most cases the governors could overrule the colonial legislatures. Needless to say, the colonists had never been happy about that.

Nonetheless, the colonists and the crown had managed to get along with each other for over a hundred and fifty years. But for the past ten years or so arguments had come up. The problem was taxes. The British government had piled up a lot of debt in fighting the French and Indian War, which had greatly benefited the Americans. The British were continuing to spend money fighting the Indians on the frontier. They thought it only fair that the Americans contributed to the expense.

Most Americans would have agreed with that. However, instead of working out a tax plan with the Americans, the English king, George III, simply announced what kind of taxes the Americans would pay, and how much. The Americans objected: they ought to have a say in it. "No taxation without representation" became their motto.

In order to get money from the colonists to help pay for the expense of British troops stationed in North America, the British government put, or levied, a tax on the kind of stamps required for various important papers. The amount of the tax was not large, but Americans objected to the principle of paying taxes they had no say in levying. Mobs seized the stamps and burned them.

A good many thoughtful Englishmen agreed with the Americans. But George III was a stubborn man, and so were many of his advisors. They viewed the Americans as children who must do as they were told.

By 1773, when Hamilton arrived in New York City, many Americans were prepared to fight for their rights. A lot of them, in fact, believed that it was time for the colonists to declare their independence from England. All over America, militias—that is, local military companies—drilled on village commons and in town squares. Farmers were hoarding gunpowder, and American leaders were making fiery speeches about the rights of Americans. Not all of them favored rebellion: perhaps a quarter or even more wanted to remain within the protection of the huge and powerful British Empire. But the majority wanted some kind of action.

As the grandson of a member of the British ruling class, Hamilton at first sided with George III and the British government. When the famous Boston Tea Party took place a few months after Hamilton had come to New York, he thought the whole thing silly. Why all this fuss about a three-penny tax on tea? He did not see that to Americans, it wasn't the tax, but the principle: did the British have a right to impose a tax without the consent of the governed?

More rioting occurred when the British government levied a tax on tea. Some Americans, partly disguised as Indians, went aboard a ship carrying tea and flung the tea chests into the water. The "Boston Tea Party" quickly became famous around the colonies. It made the British more determined than ever to put the American colonists in their place.

In any case, Hamilton was primarily concerned with his schoolwork and didn't have much time for politics. He had first to get through the equivalent of high school. With his brilliant mind and ability to work hard he caught up with his schoolmates in a few months. Then he went on to King's College in New York City (now Columbia University).

He was also, once again, trying to meet important people. As an aristocrat by blood, he felt he belonged in the same class as wealthy and highborn Americans. His sponsors back in St. Croix knew some of the leading figures in New York and New Jersey. Hamilton introduced himself to them, and inevitably he impressed them as a youth with a great future.

Conversations with such people helped to open Hamilton's eyes to the injustices Americans felt they were suffering. At college, too, he met students who felt intensely about their right to independence. Hamilton listened to these arguments and was soon won over. We should not be surprised. He was a proud young man who liked his own independence: it was in his nature to take the revolutionary side. He soon joined one of the volunteer companies training to fight the English. In a short while he became a captain of artillery. At the same time he began writing newspaper articles arguing in favor of the American position.

Matters were coming to a head. In 1775 the British, to punish the Americans for the tea party, occupied Boston with their troops. In April they marched out of the city to capture some munitions the patriots had stored at nearby Concord. An American militia met them at Lexington. Shots were fired—it is not sure who fired first. Eventually the British were driven back to Boston by Americans firing from houses, from behind walls and trees. The American Revolution was on.

The colonies organized themselves under a loose government headed not by a president, but by the Continental Congress. In time a sort of constitution, the Articles of Confederation, was drawn up. This described how the government should work and what its powers were. The Congress quickly appointed a Virginia military hero, George Washington, to command the army.

Washington realized that the British would try to take New York, which had an excellent natural harbor and was connected to the inland by the majestic Hudson River. He moved his troops to New York. The British beat the Americans and took New York, which they would hold for most of the war. Captain Hamilton was able to slip his little artillery company up along the Hudson River to the northern end of Manhattan, where Washington was pulling his army together. Here Hamilton met by chance Nathanael Greene, one of Washington's best generals. Like so many others, Greene was impressed by the young artillery captain and asked him to join his staff. But Hamilton, ever afraid of a dependency, wanted to remain independent, and so decided to stay with his artillery company.

Washington's troops once again retreated north of the city; Hamilton's company went with them. The Americans were again defeated, and retreated across the Hudson and down through New Jersey. The British chased the American troops, but could not catch them. Eventually the British gave up and returned to New York. Winter was coming; armies in those days avoided fighting in winter if they could. Washington could breathe easily for awhile. He settled in near Philadelphia, where the Continental Congress was headquartered. But the string of defeats had left Americans wondering if they could beat the British after all. Their spirits were drooping. If Americans lost heart they might give up the fight and stick with the British Empire after all. Washington knew he had to give the Americans a victory.

After the defeat of the Americans by the British on Long Island, Washington was forced to pull his troops out of New York. The British took over the city and held it through the Revolution. Unfortunately, shortly after Washington left, a great fire broke out, which destroyed some three hundred buildings.

Chapter 3

A NEW JOB

WASHINGTON'S ARMY WAS ENCAMPED on the west side of the Delaware River, north of Philadelphia. Not far away, enemy troops were quartered in the town of Trenton, New Jersey, on the other side of the river. These were not British troops, but Hessians—mercenary troops hired by George III from the German principality of Hesse. Washington decided to make a surprise attack on Trenton. He would make it on Christmas morning, when the Hessians would be tired from Christmas Eve parties and would not be expecting an attack.

An artist's idea of Alexander Hamilton in the uniform of an artillery officer, standing by a cannon pointing out of the fortifications.

On Christmas Eve Washington marched his troops to the Delaware River under cover of darkness. A cold wind blew, and by midnight a mixture of snow and sleet slashed into the faces of the shivering soldiers. At the river the men were slowly loaded into long boats, which would be poled across the Delaware. The river was now filled with chunks of floating ice, which kept getting in the way of the poles, slowing the crossing. But bit by bit the soldiers were ferried across the river, where they huddled together trying to stay warm in the storm.

Hamilton and his company were among them. The boats were growing slippery with ice and snow, and getting the cannon in and out of them was difficult. Horses skidded and fell. But they made it across.

The troops now had to march eight miles into Trenton. At three in the morning they started off, Hamilton's company along with the rest. Once again the going was slow. The plan had been to attack at daybreak, but because of the storm they were running late. However, the storm covered their movements.

A pale light was seeping through the falling snow when Hamilton first heard firing ahead. Soon the cannoneers came to a street that ran through the center of Trenton. Hamilton was ordered to fire down it. There was gunfire coming from the town, but it was difficult to see what was happening through the blowing snow. Then a detachment of Hessians rounded a corner into the street. They began firing at Hamilton's cannoneers. The cannon boomed. Hessians dropped into the snow, their bodies quickly becoming white mounds. Those still standing disappeared down an alley.

Next there appeared some Hessian cannon. Once again Hamilton's cannon blasted. Hessians went down, and the survivors fled. Hamilton's men charged the Hessian cannon and swung them around to point at the enemy. Soon the Hessians were surrendering in the streets, and it was over. The Americans had won a complete victory, capturing over nine hundred men, a thousand guns, and six Hessian cannon. Washington's army marched out of Trenton, recrossed the Delaware, and settled back into their camp, their spirits higher than they had been for months.

But Washington was not through. A few days later he once more crossed into New Jersey, this time to attack an enemy garrison at Princeton. Here again victory was complete. Hamilton was part of the Princeton fight, too.

The Battle of Princeton. The red-coated Hessians appear to be winning in this picture, but in fact they were quickly defeated.

During the battle some British occupied a building belonging to the College of New Jersey (now Princeton University). A cannonball fired by the Americans flew through a window of the college and tore the head off a portrait of George II, the previous English king. Legend has it that Hamilton's cannon fired the ball, but there is no proof one way or another.

Washington now went into winter quarters in New Jersey, and there was a lull in the fighting. Washington was determined to make improvements to his army. Among other things, he wanted to build up his staff. The commander of an army needed a lot of young helpers around to do many jobs. The aides were supposed to take care of details, like finding places for staff headquarters, reading reports from officers in the field, and helping with battle

plans. One of the biggest tasks was writing. Everything, from major reports and battle plans to the smallest order, had to be written out by hand. Then a copy had to be made for the headquarters' files. A commander counted on aides who were quick-witted and knew how he wanted things to be done. The commander needed to be able to say, "Tell

General So-and-So I want him to do such-and-such," and the aide could draw up a clear and precise order.

We do not know exactly how Washington asked Hamilton to be one of his aides. Hamilton had impressed General Greene and at least one other general that we know of. Apparently there had been talk among the top officers about this brilliant young captain who had shown coolness under fire at Trenton. Perhaps Greene recommended Hamilton. Whatever the case, Washington asked Hamilton to become one of his aides.

Nathanael Greene was one of Washington's best generals. He played an important role in the victory at Trenton and eventually commanded the American army in the South. His generalship was important to the defeat of the British in the South. Greene was one of the first in the army to recognize Hamilton's brilliance.

Hamilton was torn. From boyhood he had wanted to become a military hero, and he could only do that in battle, not on the headquarters staff where he would mostly be removed from the fighting. Furthermore, he did not want to get into a "personal dependence," which might happen to a general's aide.

On the other hand, as aide to Washington he would be at the heart of events likely to be of great historical importance, which they turned out to be. He would be close to a man who was already being considered one of the key figures of the time. So Hamilton decided to accept.

For him it had been an astonishingly rapid rise. Only four years before he had been an obscure, ill-educated teenaged clerk in an export firm on a small island in the West Indies. Now, at the age of twenty, he was at the center of events. Truly, his rise had been based on ability and hard work. Not surprisingly, Hamilton felt that he deserved his new position.

A commander and his aides were in those days called a "family." In a way, they were. They lived together, worked together, ate meals together, often shared beds in the cramped quarters they frequently lived in. Hamilton made close friends with the other aides, who called him "Ham," or "Hammy." Very quickly Washington came to trust and depend on him. Alexander Hamilton was one of those rare people who is good at both handling details and seeing the big picture.

His method was to study the details until the whole shape emerged in his mind. He was usually able very quickly to see through to the bottom of a problem and find the best way out. Later in the war he proved even more valuable: when the French came in on the American side Washington often sent him as an emissary to French commanders.

As Washington's aide and sometimes spokesman, Hamilton was able to speak to leading generals, senators, important businessmen on an equal basis. With his keen sense that he deserved to be at the highest level of society, he was never awed by important people, but treated them as his equals.

But despite the high position he had achieved, Hamilton still wanted to gain glory in battle, and occasionally he got the chance. Once, when the British were threatening Philadelphia, where the Continental Congress was at work, Washington learned that a lot of flour was about to fall into British hands. He sent Hamilton with a small group of troops to burn the flour.

The flour was stored at a mill on the banks of the Schuylkill River near Philadelphia. Coming over a rise, Hamilton saw the mill. He left two men as lookouts and with the rest rode down to the mill at the river bank. He and most of the men dismounted, preparing to burn the flour. Two barges were moored nearby. Hamilton ordered one of them to be brought up as a means of escape if necessary.

Just then he heard shots. Looking up, he saw a large force of British soldiers appear over the hill and begin to charge down on him. Quickly he ordered the men into the barge, and they began to maneuver it away from the riverbank. But the British were on them, and began firing. Hamilton's horse was shot and a man was killed. Hamilton dove into the water and swam across the river. He clambered out, found a scrap of dry paper and a pencil. Hastily he scrawled a note on his own authority to Congress: the British were close to Philadelphia and Congress must get out. It was a bold thing for an aide to tell Congress what to do, but as it happened the British were even closer to Philadelphia than Hamilton had realized. Although in the end the British did not storm Philadelphia, the danger had been quite real.

An American soldier loads his musket. This process was called "loading by the nine times" because there were nine steps to prepare a musket for firing.

The war dragged on inconclusively. Washington, who was a slow, methodical thinker, and asked everybody's opinion before making a decision—usually the correct one—had come to the conclusion that the British could not win so long as the Americans did not cave in. The British could take this city, this river, even portions of this or that state. But they could not occupy all thirteen colonies at once. There was no way for the British to win, unless the Americans beat themselves. Washington's plan was to keep his army together, duck and dodge, make hit-and-run attacks, and wait for the right time to unleash a killing blow. With this plan, the war was bound to be slow unfolding.

Then, in 1778 the French, long rivals of the British, decided to help the Americans. They sent troops and a fleet of ships. They were slow to get into the action, though, and refused to take orders from Washington: they would fight as they thought best. For some time the French troops were not much help, although the French government supplied money.

By 1780 the British, under General Cornwallis, had begun to concentrate on the South. Cornwallis believed that if he could harass the southern states enough, southerners would tire of the war and ask for peace. Without the South, the North would soon have to give up.

Cornwallis thus began moving through the southern states causing damage where he could. American forces in the South could hit at him here and there, but were not large enough for an open battle. At one point Cornwallis's troops raced in on the Virginia government, captured some of the legislators, and sent Virginia governor Thomas Jefferson fleeing into the hills. It was a humiliating defeat for the Americans.

The French decided it was time to take on Cornwallis. Washington was opposed: he believed that a combined French and American attack on New York could drive the British from the city and deprive them of a major base with a good port. But the French had made up their minds, and there was nothing Washington could do but go along.

That fall Cornwallis moved his troops into the small city of Yorktown, which backed up on the York River. The French and American troops closed in. Cornwallis believed that a British fleet would soon come up the York River, and carry his troops to safety.

But instead, a French fleet arrived, and blocked off Cornwallis's escape. Now the French and American cannon started to hammer at Yorktown. For two weeks the bombardment went on. Outside the city itself stood two redoubts—small forts guarding the city's defensive walls.

Washington, with some French officers and soldiers during the siege of Yorktown. The French, who had not done much fighting up to this point, played a major role in defeating the British in this crucial battle.

These had to be taken. Alexander Hamilton, as ever eager for military glory, begged Washington to let him command the force which would take one of the redoubts. Washington did not want to risk him, but finally he gave in.

At night Hamilton placed his men in a trench. He told them they would fight with bayonets only, the most risky kind of attack. They waited until early morning, when it was still dark. When the signal to attack came Hamilton sent twenty men out to lead the attack. He jumped out in front of them, and they staggered off through the dark, tripping on rocks and tumbling into shell holes. As they came upon the first redoubt the defenders began to fire. The Americans gave a yell and charged. They clambered over the walls, jabbing with their bayonets. Hamilton was among the first into the redoubt. In ten minutes the British defenders began to surrender and soon it was all over. Hamilton had shown great coolness and bravery under fire. Here, finally, was at least a taste of military glory.

Chapter 4

MAKING A NEW GOVERNMENT

THE VICTORY AT YORKTOWN DID NOT actually end the Revolution: a peace treaty was not signed until 1783. However, with Yorktown the fighting largely stopped. For Hamilton, the war was over.

A portrait of Alexander Hamilton when he was Washington's secretary of the treasury, by the noted painter John Trumbull.

Betsey Schuyler, Hamilton's wife, was not a great beauty, but she was from a wealthy and aristocratic family, the sort Hamilton had always aspired to join. She loved and admired her husband and kept his memory alive after his death.

He had recently married Betsey Schuyler, the daughter of a very rich American aristocrat. Betsey's father owned a huge estate near Albany, New York. Alex could have retired to the estate and lived a life of leisure, occupying himself by looking after the estate. That, however, was not Hamilton's way. He did not want to get into a dependent relationship. He wanted to earn his own money and be free to go his own way.

So he made a quick study of law, as only he could, and soon was working as a lawyer in New York City. The city was behind both Boston and Philadelphia in wealth and importance, but was rapidly catching up. With its fine natural harbor and link to inland areas via the Hudson, it was a funnel through which goods from all over the Northeast could pour out to the world. Beef, whiskey, furs, timber, cattle, and much else flooded through the city. The streets teemed with sailors speaking dozens of languages, rich men's carriages, the wheelbarrows of fish sellers, cows, and pigs being driven to market. It was an exciting place to be.

But the new nation faced a lot of problems. For one, it owed huge sums of money to all sorts of people, particularly for wartime expenses. The government was in debt to the men who served in the army, in debt to the farmers who had supplied flour and beef, in debt to munitions makers for gunpowder and guns, in debt to Americans and foreign governments alike for money it had borrowed. How were these debts to be paid?

The British still had troops around the Great Lakes, which they refused to remove until certain debts were paid. Indians were causing trouble on the frontiers. The Spanish, who controlled the Gulf Coast, had closed the mouth of the Mississippi. The so-called Barbary pirates operating in the Mediterranean were seizing American trading vessels.

One of the biggest problems George Washington's new government had to face was frontier warfare with Indians. During the early 1790s, the Indians defeated Americans troops and raided frontier settlements, sometimes killing women and children.

In 1794 General "Mad" Anthony Wayne finally crushed the Indians. In the fighting, Indian villages were burned, as shown in this picture.

These problems could have been solved by a firm government, but the national, or federal, government was not firm. The Articles of Confederation, under which the government tried to work, had some serious flaws in it. For one, each state had one vote in the Continental Congress. The big states, like Massachusetts and Virginia, resented the fact that they could be outvoted by small states like Delaware and Rhode Island, with much smaller populations. For another, the Continental Congress had no real power over the states. It could *ask* the states to pay money to the national treasury or to follow certain rules of government, but it couldn't *force* them to do it. As a result, very often the decisions of Congress were ignored by the states, and the federal government was often left without money to carry on business, much less pay off the huge debt.

A good deal of the problem lay in the fact that most Americans continued to think of themselves as citizens of their states rather than of the nation as a whole. They were Virginians, New Yorkers, or Georgians before they were Americans. Washington had early been aware of this problem. As head of the national army he had come to think "continentally"—that is, as an American rather than as a Virginian, although his home state remained dear to him. And some of the men who had served in the national army with men from other states had come to think continentally, too. But most Americans did not, and they were not sure they wanted a national government telling their home state what to do.

But thoughtful people knew that if each state continued to ignore the Congress, the federal government would soon fall apart. The individual states would be easy targets for powerful European nations.

Alexander Hamilton considered himself a New Yorker. He had been sponsored by members of a New York firm, he had gone to college in New York City, had joined a New York militia. But he had not grown up in New York, and his ties to the state were not strong. Like Washington, he had come to think continentally during the years of the war.

Moreover, Hamilton by nature distrusted ordinary human beings. Undoubtedly this feeling came from his upbringing: neither his father nor his mother had been very reliable. Furthermore, many of the people he had dealt with in the West Indies had been drifters, gamblers, or outright criminals. Hamilton believed strongly that people needed a firm hand over them. He thus wanted to see strength in government—and the Continental Congress was far from strong.

Hamilton was hardly alone in being troubled by the weakness of the federal government. Washington had spent the war years struggling to get Congress to give him what he needed to fight the war. James Madison, the brilliant Virginian scholar, was also concerned, as were others. These people were in touch with each other. Many of them, like Hamilton and Madison, were in Congress, where they met almost every day. There was much talk among them about what ought to be done to improve the federal government. The impetuous Hamilton wanted to call a convention to change the Articles of Confederation, but the others knew that public opinion would be against it. They would have to move slowly.

James Madison, a brilliant thinker, produced many of the ideas discussed at the Constitutional Convention. Although much of what he wanted was rejected, he was a key person in creating the Constitution, which means so much to us today. Paradoxically, he later tried to limit the powers of the government he had helped to bring about.

These people—Madison, Hamilton, and others—decided to set up a meeting of people from all the states to discuss commercial questions that concerned everybody. The meeting was to be held at Annapolis, Maryland. When the time came seven states sent no delegates. It was therefore impossible for the delegates to decide anything. However, they used their time to plan for another convention that would aim to revise the Articles of Confederation. It was set for May 1787.

There was no certainty that all states—or indeed any of them—would send delegates. However, the "nationalists," like Hamilton and Madison, made sure that their own states sent them. And in May of that year, the delegates trickled in. In the end, all but Rhode Island were represented at what has since been known as the Constitutional Convention, one of the most important meetings in history.

Benjamin Franklin in a brown suit and Alexander Hamilton in blue meeting over tea in the summer of 1787 when the Constitution was being written. Delegates were sworn to secrecy about the debates, and the two men had to be careful about what they said in a public place like this.

The men at the convention were surprisingly young—Hamilton himself was only thirty. However, life was shorter in those days, and there was more room at the top for younger men. Most of them were experienced politicians; many of them were lawyers; many had fought in the Revolution. They were thus realistic men, not given to chasing after fanciful ideals. They believed they knew what human beings were like, and wanted to make a government suited to what people were, not what they ought to be.

Near the beginning of the Convention, Alexander Hamilton made what some people have considered his greatest speech. Hamilton had always admired the British system. He believed that America ought to have a similar one. Inevitably, Hamilton's plan called for a very strong central government. In his plan the executive (or president) would serve for life, like the British king. There would be senators who would also serve for life, like the members of the British House of Lords as it was then. In the Hamilton plan the federal government would have most of the power; the states would have very little.

Notes in Hamilton's hand for his famous speech at the Convention. He begins by noting "Objections to the present confederation," which include the "power of treaty without power of execution" and "power to contract debts without the power to pay."

1 — Objections to the present confederation

I   Entrust the great interests of the nation to hands
    incapable of managing them —

        ~~Treaties of all kind~~

        All matters in which foreigners are concerned —

        The care of the public peace : Debts

        Power of treaty without power of execution

        Common defence without power to raise troops
        have a fleet — raise money

        — Power to contract debts without the power
        to pay —

        — These great interests of the state must be
        well managed or the public prosperity
        must be the victim —
        Legislates upon communities
        where the legislatures are to act they
        will deliberate —
                                        { To ask money or
                                        { & by after unjust
                                          to act
        No sanction —

989

Hamilton's speech was highly praised by everyone. However, no one but Hamilton himself supported it. Americans had just fought a revolution to get rid of a tyrannical government; why should they saddle themselves with another one? Then, too, as a practical matter, the delegates to the convention realized that the American people would never accept the plan Hamilton proposed.

But Hamilton's speech was important, for it encouraged the other delegates to think boldly: don't just tinker with the Articles of Confederation, but scrap it altogether and build something new.

That is what the delegates eventually did. Instead of revising the Articles, they created a new constitution, which has proven to be one of the most significant documents ever written. Without our Constitution, the free, prosperous, and powerful United States

An artist's idea of Washington presiding at the Constitutional Convention. Actually, as president, Washington rarely spoke in the debates but got his opinions across after-hours in private meetings with the delegates.

of today would probably not exist, and the history of the world would have been vastly different.

The men at the Constitutional Convention, however, could not put the new Constitution into effect on their own say-so. It had to be ratified—that is, approved—by nine states before it went into effect. It was not at all certain that the American people would approve it. Indeed, when it was first published for all to see, it is probable that a majority of Americans opposed it. They were still worried about setting up a tyrannical government like the one they had just got rid of at the cost of so many lives.

The nationalists knew this, and they started a vigorous campaign to change public opinion. Hamilton was one of the foremost in doing this in his own state. He knew that if an important state like New York failed to ratify the new Constitution there was a good chance it would sink. He was by no means completely satisfied with the Constitution. However, he knew that if it was not approved the country would go on being run by the sorry Articles of Confederation and was likely to break up.

So he suggested to some other nationalists that they write a series of newspaper articles in support of the Constitution. These famous articles are now known as *The Federalist* papers.

Although Hamilton talked to a number of people about contributing to *The Federalist* papers, in the end they were written by James Madison, John Jay, and Hamilton himself. Historians are still not sure exactly which of these three wrote which articles. However it is agreed that Hamilton wrote the first introductory article and about two-thirds of the rest.

Hamilton's writing in *The Federalist* papers is brilliant. He reined back his normal impetuosity. The writing is quiet and calm, the arguments carefully laid out. Again and again he showed why this or that had to be in the Constitution—why different ideas would not work. *The Federalist* papers are among a handful of basic American documents, along with the Declaration of Independence and the Constitution itself. They are still frequently quoted by judges to show what the Constitution is supposed to mean. They did not by themselves convince Americans to ratify the Constitution; but they provided ammunition and arguments for its supporters, not just in New York State, but in all thirteen states. And the following year, in 1788, the Constitution was ratified.

The Federalist *papers are among the most important four or five documents in American history. For one, they are filled with strong arguments for agreeing to the new Constitution. For another, they are still used today by lawyers and judges to help them decide what the Founding Fathers meant by this or that part of the Constitution.*

THE

FEDERALIST:

ADDRESSED TO THE

PEOPLE OF THE STATE OF NEW-YORK.

NUMBER I.

Introduction.

AFTER an unequivocal experience of the ineffi-cacy of the subsisting federal government, you are called upon to deliberate on a new constitution for the United States of America. The subject speaks its own importance; comprehending in its consequences, nothing less than the existence of the UNION, the safety and welfare of the parts of which it is com-posed, the fate of an empire, in many respects, the most interesting in the world. It has been frequently remarked, that it seems to have been reserved to the people of this country, by their conduct and example, to decide the important question, whether societies of men are really capable or not, of establishing good government from reflection and choice, or whether they are forever destined to depend, for their political constitutions, on accident and force. If there be any truth in the remark, the crisis, at which we are arrived, may with propriety be regarded as the æra in which

A   that

Chapter 5
BUILDING A NATION

THE COUNTRY NOW HAD A CONSTITUTION. It now needed a government. It had been expected all along that George Washington would be elected president easily, and he was. John Adams of Massachusetts was elected vice president.

Washington knew that, no matter how carefully a constitution was worked out, it could not anticipate every problem a government would face.

A French drawing shows Washington being informed of his election as first president of the United States. The drawing was made in 1789, as the great French Revolution was beginning. The example of the American victory against the British was important in inspiring the French to throw off their rulers.

The new president and his officials would have to make a lot of decisions about how the government should work and what it could do. These decisions would set patterns and policies that would affect the nation for years, if not centuries. For example, Washington decided to step down after two terms as president, although he could have been elected for a third term if he had wished. Thereafter all presidents followed this precedent until 1940, when Franklin D. Roosevelt was elected for a third term. Soon after, the Constitution was changed to prohibit third terms.

Washington wanted the best, wisest people he could find for his cabinet. The federal government was tiny compared to what it is today. Washington had only a few cabinet officers to appoint. He chose his old friend from Virginia, Thomas Jefferson, who had been an emissary to France, as his secretary of state. An equally important office was secretary of the treasury. Whoever held this post would have to deal with the problem of the huge governmental debt piled up during the war. Who should Washington name? He went to Robert Morris, who had run finances for the old government. According to one story, he asked, "What are we to do with this heavy debt?" Morris replied, "There is but one man who can tell you; that is Alexander Hamilton."

It was probably the advice Washington wanted to hear. He knew that Hamilton was proud and impetuous.

He also knew that Hamilton was brilliant, and despite his impulsiveness, would always study a problem carefully before acting. So, Hamilton became our first secretary of the treasury.

Hamilton was going to be a major figure in starting the United States off in a new direction. We can point to three actions he made that continue to affect us today.

One of these sprung out of the huge debt owed by both state and federal governments to all sorts of people. In those days, as strange as it may see, there was

An engraving of Hamilton meant for sale to the public. It was probably issued following Hamilton's death in 1804.

little actual money around. There was no such thing as paper money; it was all in coins.

Most ordinary people lived largely by barter. Ninety percent of Americans lived on farms. They made almost everything they needed. They spun cotton and wool for thread, wove thread into cloth, sewed cloth into shirts and dresses. They butchered their own cows, hogs, and chickens, grew their own vegetables and fruit, made their own cider and candles, built their own houses and barns. What little they needed from outside they charged at the local store. When the harvest was in they would clear the debt with so many barrels of apples, cider, wheat, salt beef. The storekeeper would then ship the produce he had collected from local farmers, usually by river, down to a big city like Philadelphia or Boston, where it was swapped for things like needles, ax heads, and plows that he sold in his store.

The work most people did to make their farms thrive was fearfully hard. In many places, especially New England, the land was filled with rocks. Farmers usually dug up the rocks and laid them along the edges of fields to make walls, but they sometimes buried large boulders in deep holes, as shown in this picture.

Because there was always a shortage of actual money, and because it was risky to send boxes of gold and silver coins on ships that might sink in a storm or be attacked by pirates, business was done on credit. Merchant Dubois in Paris might owe a thousand *livres* to merchant Smith in London, who in turn owed five hundred pounds to Merchant Rodgers in New York. Such merchants continually swapped these credits around among themselves to balance things out.

Needless to say, everybody in this system had to have absolute trust in everybody else. This was especially true of government. Hamilton was aware of that fact. He believed strongly that the new American government must establish trust with the world by paying off the huge war debts.

But Hamilton had more in mind than just showing the world that American credit was good. He believed that the future of America lay not with farming, but with industry. At the time, the economics of most countries was based on farming. However, a few nations were beginning to *industrialize*—that is, they were learning how to make with machines what people had always made with their hands. This was particularly true of England, which was leading the so-called Industrial Revolution. There, for example, clever men had devised machines for spinning wool into thread and weaving thread into cloth. Factories, driven by waterpower, were being built, and industrialists were growing rich.

Hamilton wanted to develop industry in the new United States. Even while he was in office, the textile industry—spinning wool and cotton into thread and weaving thread into cloth—was starting up. Here, machines spin thread.

Hamilton believed that America ought to follow this path. However, building factories and filling them with machines took money. Hamilton decided that the government ought to create a class of wealthy people who had money to invest in new businesses. He worked out a scheme for paying off the debt that would put a lot of money in the hands of a relatively few people—usually people who already had a good deal of money.

This plan was not very democratic, but Hamilton, remember, had grown up thinking of himself as an aristocrat and had married into an aristocratic family. He believed it was more important to build American industry than to be strictly fair; in the long run, he said, everybody would benefit from an industrial America.

Some of Washington's advisors were strongly opposed to Hamilton's scheme. Among them were Jefferson and James Madison. They believed that people in industrial societies who lived in cities were not nearly as honest and decent as those who lived in the country. Americans would be happier and more virtuous if they stuck to farming. Let the corrupt European nations, with their dirty, vice-ridden cities, make manufactured goods, which Americans could buy with the profits from their farm products.

Thomas Jefferson, third president and primary writer of the Declaration of Independence, opposed Hamilton's ideas for a strong central government and industrialization. But when Jefferson became president, he proved to be a strong president of the kind Hamilton had wanted.

In the end Washington agreed with Hamilton. The government set up Hamilton's plan for paying off the debt, which allowed some people to become wealthy. In fact, these people did not immediately begin to invest in new factories as Hamilton had hoped. But over time America became industrialized and grew enormously prosperous. Hamilton had been right. Some people today like to think that Hamilton founded American capitalism. The story is far more complicated than that, but it explains why Hamilton's statue stands at the heart of New York's financial district.

Perhaps an even more important idea of Hamilton's was the establishment of "implied powers" as basic to government. This idea first became important when Hamilton decided that the country needed a national bank. Such a bank would help control the country's finances. It would also lend money to people who wanted to start new businesses, thus giving industrialization another push.

There was a lot of opposition to the national bank, especially among people like Jefferson and Madison, who wanted to keep the country a nation of virtuous farmers. In arguing against Hamilton's bank, Madison said, "Reviewing the Constitution, it is not possible to discover in it the power to incorporate a bank." In Madison's opinion, then, if the Constitution did not specifically give the government the right to do something, it could not do it.

Hamilton's argument was based on a clause in the Constitution that the government could do anything that was "necessary and proper" to doing its work. For example, the Constitution did not specifically authorize the government to order guns for soldiers; but the Constitution did give the government the power to "provide for the common defense" of the country and "to raise and support armies." Buying guns was certainly "necessary and proper" to building an army for the defense of the country and was thus allowed under the Constitution.

That much everyone could agree with. But Hamilton went farther. He argued that *necessary* did not mean simply "needful," as most people would define the word. It meant that the government could do anything that might be "helpful" to jobs the government must do. The government had the power to "regulate commerce." A national bank would help to regulate commerce and it was therefore allowable under the "necessary and proper" clause of the Constitution.

It all came down to how you defined *necessary*. Hamilton, as we know, believed in a very strong government. He also believed that people needed to have a firm hand over them. It is therefore not surprising that he wanted to stretch the meaning of the Constitution as far as he could.

George Washington, while not going as far as Hamilton, also believed in a strong central government. He had suffered mightily during the Revolution under a government that never gave him the tools he needed to defeat the British. He would lean toward strength. He sided with Hamilton, and this broad definition of the "necessary and proper" clause became basic to the American system. Historians agree that Hamilton and Washington were right, for their interpretation of the "necessary and proper" clause has allowed the federal government to do all sorts of important things that the Founding Fathers could not have imagined, like setting up safety regulations for airplanes, establishing pollution controls, building national parks, giving young people college scholarships. Alexander Hamilton did not invent this interpretation. But he was the one who made it basic to American policy. Later on, the Supreme Court agreed with him.

Finally, Hamilton was a key figure in starting the two-party system under which American politics has operated ever since. However, he did not do it on purpose. Nearly all of the Founding Fathers, including Hamilton, hated the whole idea of political parties, which they called "factions." They were very familiar with the English party system, then dominated by the Whigs and the Tories. They believed that in England and elsewhere, party members usually put the interests of their parties ahead of the interests of their country. They also felt that political parties corrupted government, because people in power invariably tried to get political jobs for their friends in their own party, even in if they were not the best choice. Everybody hoped that the United States could do without political parties.

But as we have seen, almost from the beginning powerful men were separating into two camps. Hamilton and his sup-porters wanted to set up a national bank, wanted a broad view of the "necessary and proper" clause, wanted to push for industrialization. Madison, Jefferson, and their followers took the opposite position on these questions and others.

As time passed these factions became more and more divided and quarrelsome. The Hamilton group came to be called the Federalists, the Jefferson/Madison group the Republicans. (This was not the present Republican party, which was founded some fifty years later.) Washington tried hard to stay neutral, and kept urging Hamilton and Jefferson, his two main cabinet officers, to work out their differences. But at heart Washington believed in a strong Federal government, and in the end he tipped toward the Federalists. The next president, John Adams, was also a Federalist, but by the election of 1800 the Republicans had gathered more people to their side, and their favorite, Thomas Jefferson, became president. He was followed by his friend and supporter, James Madison.

But in the end Hamilton and Washington won. By the time Thomas Jefferson was chosen president, the Federalists had been in power for twelve years. They had firmly established the idea that the federal government would be relatively strong. When the Republicans took over, they did little to reduce the power of the federal government. In fact, many important things Jefferson and Madison did might not have been permitted under a strict interpretation of the "necessary and proper" clause. Ever since, the federal government has felt able to do what it had to do for the good of the country. Most historians believe that the broad interpretation of the "necessary and proper" clause has been important to making America the prosperous and powerful nation it is today.

With the end of Washington's second term, Hamilton's major work was done. He continued to practice law, but unfortunately he got caught up in a scandal, which damaged his reputation. Not long after, in 1804, he was challenged to a duel by a disappointed politician Hamilton had opposed named Aaron Burr. Foolishly, Hamilton accepted the challenge. He was killed in the duel.

But his legacy was immense. There is no question that Alexander Hamilton was a critically important figure in the creation of the United States. He played a role in the Revolution, an important part in writing the Constitution, and a key role in the first government under the new Constitution. Of the Founding Fathers, only those who became president, like Adams and Jefferson, were more important. It is possible to argue that in the long term, Hamilton was more significant than any but Washington himself.

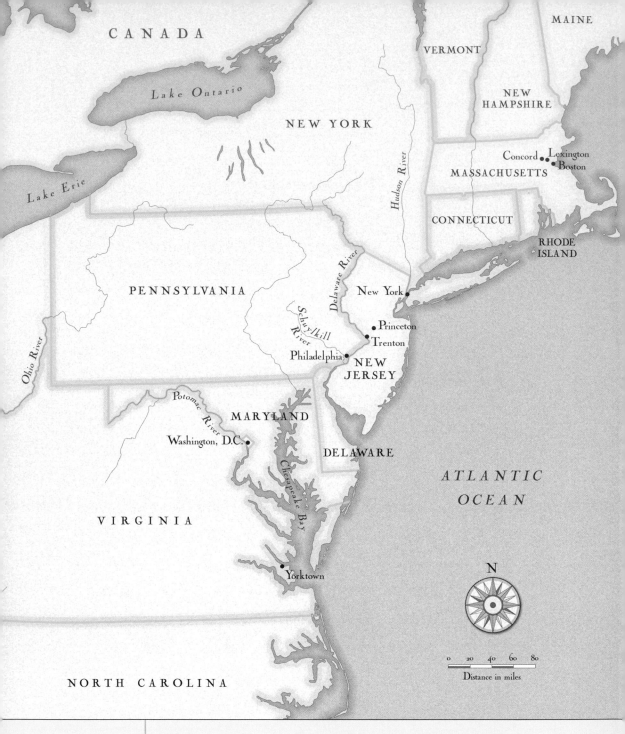

This map shows the sites of the major Revolutionary War battles in which Alexander Hamilton took part.

Author's Note on Sources

The main scholarly works on Hamilton are *Alexander Hamilton: A Concise Biography*, by Broadus Mitchell, *The Young Hamilton: A Biography*, by James Thomas Flexner, and *Alexander Hamilton: A Biography*, by Forrest McDonald. There are fewer works for children. One is *Alexander Hamilton*, by Mollie Keller.

Keller, Millie. *Alexander Hamilton*. New York: Franklin Watts, 1986. (young readers)

McDonald, Forrest. *Alexander Hamilton: A Biography*. New York: W.W. Norton, 1979.

Rosenburg, John. *Alexander Hamilton: America's Bold Lion*. Brookfield, CT: The Millbrook Press, 2000. (young readers)

INDEX

(wife), 50, *50*
Hamilton, James (brother), 14
Hamilton, James (father),
12–14, 16
Hamilton, Rachel (mother),
12, 14, 16, 18, 19, 21
Hessians, 35, 37–38

Implied powers, 71
industrialization, 67–71, 74

Jay, John, 60
Jefferson, Thomas, 45, 64,
69, *69*, 71, 74, 75

King's College in New York
City, 31

Lesser Antilles, 6–7

Madison, James, 54, *54*, 55,
60, 69, 71, 74
maps, 7, *76*
Morris, Robert, 64

National bank, 71
Nevis, 12
"necessary and proper," 71–75
New Jersey, 31, 33, 38–39

New York, 27, 29, 31, 32–33,
50, 53

Philadelphia, 33, 42–43
preferment, *22*

Republicans, 74

St. Croix, *11*, 16, 23–26, 31
sugar, 8, *9*, 10, *20*

Taxes, 27–29
tobacco, 8, 24
Tories, 73
two-party system, 73

U.S. Constitution, 58–61,
71–72, 75
U.S. Supreme Court, 73

Washington, George, 6, 15,
18, 32–33, 35–47, 52–54, *59*,
62, 63–64, 70, 72, 74
Wayne, "Mad" Anthony, *51*
West Indies, 8, 14, 41
wharves, *10*
Whigs, 73

Yorktown, 45–47, 49

ABOUT THE AUTHOR

James Lincoln Collier has written many books, both fiction and nonfiction, for children and adults. His interests span history, biography, and historical fiction. He is an authority on the history of jazz and performs weekly on the trombone in New York City.

My Brother Sam Is Dead was named a Newbery Honor Book and a Jane Addams Honor Book and was a finalist for a National Book Award. *Jump Ship to Freedom* and *War Comes to Willy Freemen* were each named a notable Children's Trade Book in the Field of Social Studies by the National Council for Social Studies and the Children's Book Council. Collier received the Christopher Award for *Decision in Philadelphia: The Constitutional Convention of 1787*. He lives in Pawling, New York.